FORCES
and
Motion
in Sports

by Glen Phelan

Table of Contents

Introduction

WHUMP! The Broncos put the volleyball in play. It clears the net. Then the ball sinks quickly toward an open spot on the court. It looks like a sure point for the Broncos. But out of nowhere, a Pirate defender dives for the ball. What a save! He bumps the ball to a teammate who pushes it high toward the net. A Pirate leaps. So do two Broncos. Will they block the shot? The Pirate swings his arm to meet the ball. SMASH! Point for the Pirates!

Volleyball is a game of **forces** and **motion**. A force is a push or a pull. Forces make things move. There are plenty of pushes and pulls in this game. There's a lot of motion, too. Motion is any change in an object's position. The volleyball is constantly changing position. So are the players. They know how to use forces and motion to play their very best.

Learning about forces and motion will help you play at the top of your game, too. This book will show you how forces and motion are at work while you are at play.

▲ The defender (left) pushes against the floor to leap high into the air.

▲ The striker (right) pushes down hard on the ball to spike it.

Different Kinds of Forces

It takes force to throw a ball. It takes force to hit a ball. And it takes force to stop a ball. Where do these forces—the pushes and pulls—come from? They start with your **muscles**.

A lot of the muscles in your body are attached to bone. The muscles pull on the bones to move your body. Take a look at the softball pitcher here. The muscles in her shoulder pull on bones in her arm. This pulling lets her raise her arm back. Other muscles pull on bones to swing her arm forward. That swinging lets her give the ball a big push—a pitch. The ball flies toward home plate.

◀ **Muscles use force to pull on bones and move your body.**

Changing Direction

The pitcher uses force to start the ball moving. Now it's the batter's turn to use force. She holds the bat shoulder high. She steps forwards and swings her arms across her waist. Dozens of muscles are pulling her bones. Then she hits the ball with the bat. WHACK!

The bat changes the direction of the ball and gives the ball a big push. This force sends the ball high into the air. What happens next?

It's a Fact

There are over 600 muscles that control how your body moves.

◀ Force from the bat pushes the ball in a new direction.

The ball sails through the air. You know that it will fall back down. But that is only because the force of **gravity** pulls it down.

Gravity is a force that pulls any two objects together. In this case, the two objects are Earth and the ball. Because Earth is so big, the pull of its gravity is strong. So no matter how high the ball is hit, it always comes back down.

Hands-on Experiment
Ball Bounce

When you drop a rubber ball, gravity pulls it down. Then it bounces. How high does it bounce? Let's find out.

What You'll Need:
- rubber ball • meter stick

What To Do

1. Set up a table like this one.

2. Have a friend hold the meter stick against a wall. The o-cm mark of the stick should touch the floor.

Height of Drop	Height of Bounce
20 cm	
40 cm	
60 cm	
80 cm	
100 cm	

3. Hold the ball near the meter stick so that the bottom of the ball is even with the 20-cm mark. Let the ball go, and see how high it bounces. Measure the height from the bottom of the ball.

4. Repeat for every 20 cm on the meter stick. Record the height of the bounce in your table.

Solve This

the ball-bounce experiment, you collected data, or information.
learn more from data, you can make a graph like the one shown here.
e the graph to predict how high the ball might bounce if dropped
m 120 cm.

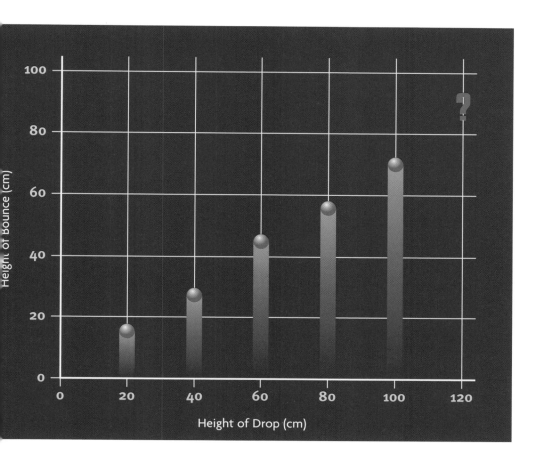

What Do You Think?
Will a ball ever bounce up to its original height?

Back at the Game

Rubber balls aren't the only balls that bounce. When gravity pulls the softball down to the ground, it bounces a few times. Each bounce gets lower and lower. Then it rolls on the ground and stops.

Did the ball slow down and stop because it ran out of force? No, things don't run out of force. Rather, other forces acted on the ball to slow it down and stop it. One of those forces is **friction**. Friction happens when one object rubs against another object. This rubbing is a push. Friction makes it harder for things to move.

Each time a ball bounces, it rubs a little bit against the ground and slows down. When a ball rolls, it rubs against the ground a lc The ball finally stops.

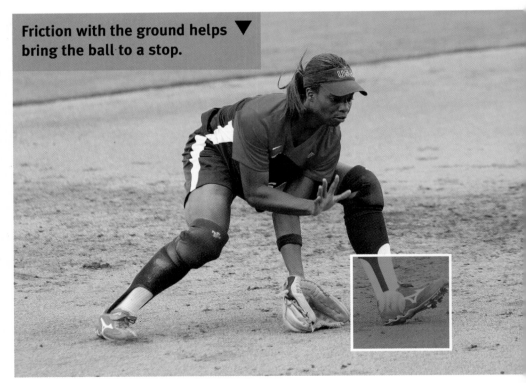

Friction with the ground helps ▼ bring the ball to a stop.

Meanwhile, the batter is racing down the first base line. She rounds the bag and heads for second. The outfielder picks up the ball and throws it to second base. The fielder throws the ball hard, but **air resistance** slows it down. Air resistance is friction between an object and gas particles in the air. The runner's hand reaches the base a split second before the ball. SAFE!

It's a Fact

There are 108 stitches on a baseball. They hold together the two pieces of leather that cover the ball. Those stitches raised above the ball's smooth surface also increase the air resistance. The spin and the increased friction cause air to press against one side of the ball more than the other. The ball curves and becomes harder to hit or catch.

▼ Friction keeps the runner from sliding past second base.

Forces and Motion in Individual Sports

Now that you know something about forces and the motions they cause, let's see how they influence other sports.

Skateboarding

Have you ever gone skateboarding on the sidewalk? Chances are, you have to keep pushing off with your leg every five or ten seconds. That's because friction between the wheels and the ground slows you down. You have to keep adding your own pushing force to overcome the force of friction. In fact, skateboarding is a constant battle against friction. Makers of skateboards use information about forces and motion to help you win that battle.

Little steel balls called ball bearings roll between the metal parts of a skateboard wheel. This reduces friction and lets the wheel roll more freely.

Ramps in skate parks are designed so that skateboarders can use gravity to help them go faster. The downward pull of gravity adds some zip to the ride.

How does gravity help ▶
this skateboarder enjoy
the ride?

ball bearings ———

Snowboarding

Does whooshing down a snow-covered hill while standing on a small board appeal to your sense of adventure? The extreme sport of snowboarding is known for its **speed**. Speed is how fast something is moving at any given moment. Speed is measured in units of distance per unit of time. For example: 30 miles (19 kilometers) per hour is how fast a snowboarder might move when zipping down the mountain!

2. Solve This

Suppose a snowboarder moves 40 meters in 5 seconds. What is the snowboarder's speed in meters per second? Hint: speed = distance/time.

▲ Snowboarders control their speed by changing direction.

Why is snowboarding such a speedy sport? One reason is gravity. The steeper the slope, or slant, of the mountain, the faster gravity pulls the snowboarder down.

Another reason for the speed is less friction. The snowboard has smooth surface. The snow is smooth, too. So there is not a lot of rubbing between the two surfaces. To further reduce the friction, some snowboarders put wax on their boards.

Going fast can be a lot of fun. But going too fast can cause crashes. How do snowboarders control their speed? They change direction. They move from side to side instead of going straight down the mountain. Digging the edge of the snowboard into the snow increases friction on one side of the board and that helps the rider turn in that direction.

A snowboarder moves at different ▶
speeds down the mountain.

▲ Many forces and motions make the pins fall.

Bowling

It all comes down to this last ball. You need a strike to score your best ever. You swing your arm back, then forward, and release the fourteen-pound (six-kilogram) bowling ball. It rolls quickly down the middle of the lane. Will it knock over all ten pins?

That depends. Did you throw a heavy enough ball with enough force? Did it hit the pins in the right spot?

If you could look at a strike in slow motion, you would see that the bowling ball hits only a few of the pins. Those pins tumble through the air and knock down other pins. For this to happen, the ball has to hit the pins with a certain amount of force.

If you choose a ball that is too heavy, you won't be able to throw with enough **velocity** (vuh-LAH-suh-tee) to make the pins umble. Velocity is speed with a direction. For instance, you might nrow the ball with a velocity of ten miles (sixteen kilometers) per our toward the pins.

But you need more than velocity. If you choose a ball that is too ght, it might not have enough **mass**, or weight, to make the pins umble. So choose a ball that is light enough to throw with control.

Tennis

The tennis ball bounces high over your head. You extend your arm up, with the head of the racket above the ball. Whap! The ball rockets over the net and lands in the corner. You win the point, game, set, and match.

Smashing a winning shot is a terrific feeling. But hitting a tennis ball out of the court can be frustrating. Use your knowledge of forces to help control your game.

Hit the ball at the highest point of its bounce. The direction of your force (the swinging racket) will be straighter. If you hit the ball as it's dropping, you tend to direct the force upward. The ball might sail out of the court.

Turn your body and step forward when you swing your arm. This will give you more power.

Follow through. That means continue your swinging motion after you hit the ball. If you stop swinging when the racket makes contact with the ball, it will move forward slowly. The ball may no have enough velocity to make it over the net.

But if you follow through, the ball will be in contact with the swinging racket longer. That will give the ball more force. And the more force the ball has, the faster and farther it will go.

Tennis players need to follow ▶ through. That gives more force to the ball and increases its velocity.

They Made a Difference

Who was the greatest scientist of all time? Many experts think it was Isaac Newton. This 17th-century scientist developed the laws of motion. Those laws explain how all objects move—whether it's a tennis ball or a planet. Newton explained what gravity is and how it works.

It's a Fact

High-speed photography shows that a tennis ball changes shape as a racket hits it. The ball flattens. The strings of the racket also change shape. Both the strings and the ball spring back into shape.

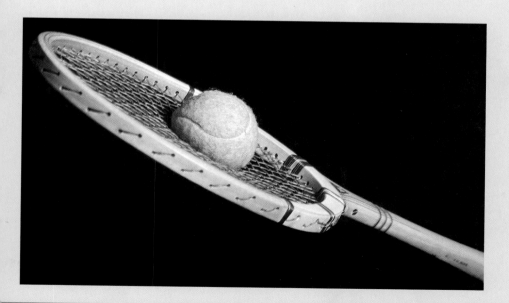

Forces and Motion in Team Sports

Which sport involves the most forces? It would probably be a team sport. American football might be the forces cham On any given play, twenty-two people are running, blocking, tackling, throwing, and more. That's a lot of pushing and pulling. But the forces are not always obvious.

Look at the football play shown here. There's plenty of action, b these two opposing players don't seem to be getting anywhere. Tha because they are pushing into each other with the same amount of force. Their forces are balanced. **Balanced forces** are equal but in opposite directions.

What happens if one player pushes with more force than the other player? The forces become unbalanced. The player with the

weaker force will get pushed back. **Unbalanced forces** result in an object moving or changing its motion.

◀ **These players don't move forward or backward because their forces are balanced.**

Momentum and Inertia

It's tough to tackle a football player, especially one who is big and fast. That's because a player with a lot of mass and velocity has a lot of **momentum** (moh-MEN-tuhm), which is the strength of an object in motion. Scientists use a math formula to calculate momentum. It is the product, or result, of its mass multiplied by its velocity (momentum = mass x velocity). The more momentum an object has, the harder it is to stop.

3. Solve This

Rank the momentum of these three players. Which one is probably easiest to bring down in a tackle?

(A) Mass: 88 kg
Velocity:
8 meters per second

(B) Mass: 93 kg
Velocity:
9 meters per second

(C) Mass: 100 kilograms
Velocity:
7 meters per second

Once an object is moving, it keeps moving unless a force acts on it. In other words, an object resists any change in its motion. Scientists call this **inertia** (ih-NUR-shuh). The picture below shows how inertia leads to a fumble.

When the player runs, both he and the ball are moving forward. Then . . . BAM! The tackler's force stops him and the ball carrier loses his grip on the ball. But no force has been applied to stop the ball. It continues to move forward because of its inertia. Then, the force of gravity causes the ball to drop to the ground. It will continue to roll until friction causes the ball to stop—or another player picks it up.

point

Think About It

How can a smaller football player get the same momentum as a larger football player?

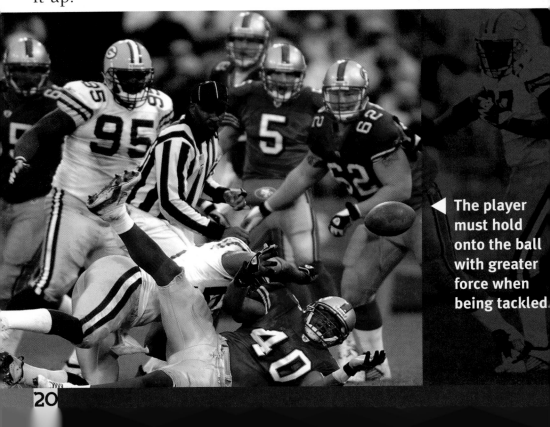

◀ The player must hold onto the ball with greater force when being tackled.

Forces on the Soccer Field

Ideas of force and motion apply to all sports. Here are some that may be familiar to you from soccer.

- Friction constantly slows the ball down as it rolls along the grassy field.
- A player will get a running start to gain momentum and kick the ball with more power.
- A player will follow through with her kick to make the ball go faster.

Another idea of motion is especially important in soccer. The goalie throws the ball by swinging her arm in a big arc. When she lets go, does the ball continue to move through the air in the curved pattern of an arc? No. When she releases the ball, she is no longer giving it a force. So the ball moves in a straight line at the point of release. Of course, gravity and air resistance act on it immediately to change its motion.

▲ How will the ball move after the goalie releases it?

Hands-on Experiment
Adjusting for Wind

Almost any sport you play outside is affected by the wind. How can you change the way you throw a ball to adjust for the force of the wind? Try this experiment.

What You'll Need
• ping-pong ball • trash can • fan with multiple speeds

What To Do
1. Place the trash can six feet (two meters) from where you are standing. Practice tossing the ping-pong ball into the can. Observe the flight path of the ball.
2. Place the fan between you and the trash can, facing the path of the ball. Turn the fan on low speed.
3. Try tossing the ball into the trash can using the same flight path you did in step 1. Is the ball blown off course?
4. Change the direction of your toss so that the ball falls in the can as the fan blows. Practice several times.
5. Repeat steps 2–4 using different fan speeds.

What Do You Think?
How did you have to change your toss to get the ball in the container?

Projectiles in Sports

Many sports, especially team sports, involve throwing a ball. A ball that is thrown is a **projectile** (pruh-JEK-tighl). As soon as you release the ball, gravity starts to pull it down. But the ball still moves forward because of the push you gave it. The combination of the forward motion and gravity makes the ball travel in an arc.

Knowing how projectiles travel is especially important when you want to sink a shot in basketball. Some people throw the ball too hard. Then it doesn't have a chance to complete its arc and fall into the basket.

▼ A basketball rises and falls in the shape of an arc.

Friction on the Ice

The hockey players skate down the ice. They pass the puck back and forth one . . . two . . . three times. The puck becomes a blur as the player slaps a shot toward the goal at 100 miles (160 kilometers) per hour.

Hockey is a fast-paced game. At first, it might look like there is no friction to slow things down. But friction happens when the high spots of rough surfaces snag on each other. Every surface, even the surface of ice and hockey pucks, has high spots to some degree. Tiny bits of the puck and ice are bumping into each other all along the way. This bumping produces friction that will eventually slow and stop the puck.

Little friction with ▶ **the ice lets the puck move quickly.**

Now let's take another look at hockey and you'll see that friction is an important force in this fast-paced sport.

Friction between the ice and metal skates creates heat that melts a tiny bit of the ice. Hockey players actually glide over this film of water when they skate.

A puck doesn't have enough space to slow down much in a hockey rink. But there's plenty of friction when the puck hits the boards or a player's stick.

A quick start and a quick stop require a lot of friction as the player digs his skates into the ice.

Hockey players wrap tape around the end of their hockey sticks. The tape has a rougher surface than the stick, so it increases friction between the stick and the puck. This gives players more control over the puck.

Hockey players and ice skaters glide on a film of water.

Forces and Motion in Water Sports

Forces and motion that happen in air also happen in water. Take a look at this dive.

The diver pushes off the board and leaps into the air. Gravity pulls her toward the water. As she enters the water, her hands form a wedge. That pushes the water aside. But friction with the water slows her down. At the bottom, she stops, then pushes off. The force sends her toward the surface.

▲ **Many forces are at work in one dive.**

Swimming

The next time you go for a swim, look at all the forces involved. You'll get a better understanding of the saying, "sink or swim."

Swimming for even a short time can be tiring. The swimmer has to push against the water in order to move. That's hard to do because there's more friction in water than in air. So more force is needed to swim through water than to walk through air. A swimmer uses hands, arms, legs, and feet to push against the water. By pushing back against the water, a swimmer moves in the opposite direction—forward. Meanwhile, the swimmer has to use enough force to fight against the force of gravity.

It's a Fact

Swimmers who race try to reduce the amount of friction between themselves and the water. Some swimmers wear a swimsuit that is made like a shark's skin. A shark's skin has tiny bumps on it that let water move around the shark quickly. That helps sharks swim fast. Swimmers hope it makes them swim faster, too.

Swimmers use ▶ their hands and feet like paddles to push against the water.

Rowing and Water Polo

"Pull! Pull!" That's what a teammate often yells out during a rowing race. What are the rowers pulling on? The oars. When the rower pulls on one end of the oar, the other end pushes against the water. Pushing in one direction sends the boat in the opposite direction.

▲ **What forces are at work in water polo?**

Forces in a rowing race are fairly simple and steady. In a game of water polo, however, the forces get a bit more complicated. Many of the forces and motions are similar to those in soccer. There are some differences, too. For example, to make a clean shot at the goal, a player has to lift himself out of the water a little. How is that done? By pushing down on the water.

▲ **Rowers know that when you push in one direction, you move in the other direction.**

Careers in Science

When you think of a career in sports, the first thing that comes to mind might be a professional athlete. But many sports careers don't include playing the game. Sports trainer is one of them. Trainers are part of the medical staff of a sports team. Trainers have lots of duties. They put protective bandages on players before the game. They treat minor injuries during and after a game. They also help athletes recover from major injuries. To be a trainer, you need a college degree in physical therapy.

 point

Talk About It

Choose a sport. Name four ways that friction and gravity are important in that sport. Share your thoughts with a partner.

Conclusion

Every sport uses forces and motion. Forces include friction, air resistance, and gravity. Some different ways to describe motion include speed, velocity, momentum, and projectiles By understanding forces and motion, you can better understand how different sports are played. You can also pick up some ideas on how to use those forces and motions to play better.

Now that you know more about forces and motion, use the chart below to explain how the volleyball players shown on page are using different forces in their game.

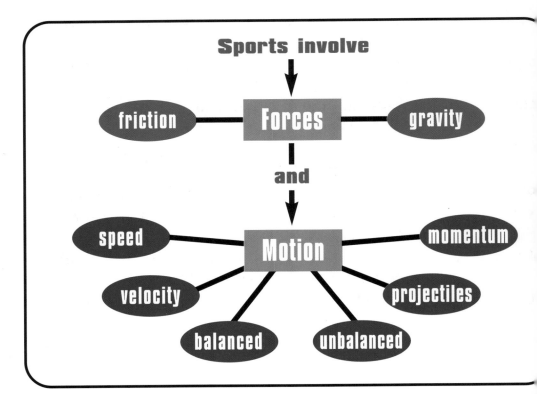

Glossary

air resistance	(AYR ri-ZIS-tuhns) friction between an object and gas particles in the air (page 9)
balanced forces	(BAL-uhnsd FOR-sus) forces that act equally on an object but in opposite directions (page 18)
force	(FORS) a push or a pull (page 2)
friction	(FRIK-shuhn) a force that happens when one object rubs against another object (page 8)
gravity	(GRAV-i-tee) a force that pulls any two objects together (page 6)
inertia	(ih-NUR-shuh) the resistance to change in an object's motion (page 20)
mass	(MAS) the quantity of matter that a body contains; weight (page 15)
momentum	(moh-MEN-tuhm) the product of an object's mass and its velocity (page 19)
motion	(MOH-shuhn) any change in an object's position (page 2)
muscle	(MUS-uhl) a tissue in the body that is made of strong fibers (page 4)
projectile	(pruh-JEK-tighl) an object that is thrown (page 23)
speed	(SPEED) how fast an object is moving at any given moment (page 12)
unbalanced forces	(un-BAL-uhnsd FOR-sus) forces that result in an object moving or changing its motion (page 18)
velocity	(vuh-LAH-suh-tee) the speed and direction of an object (page 15)

Index

Solve This Answers

1. Page 7
Approximately 82 cm

2. Page 12
8 meters per second

3. Page 19
Momentum is determined by multiplying mass times velocity. The values of the momentums are:
Player A: 704 meters/second;
Player B: 837 meters/second;
Player C: 700 meters/second.
The easiest player to bring down would be Player C because he has the least momentum.